UNDER THE HOOD
THE HISTORY OF ALFA ROMEOS

SETH HINGSTON

NEW YORK

Published in 2019 by The Rosen Publishing Group, Inc.
29 East 21st Street, New York, NY 10010

Copyright © 2019 by The Rosen Publishing Group, Inc.

All rights reserved. No part of this book may be reproduced in any form without permission in writing from the publisher, except by a reviewer.

First Edition

Editor: Elizabeth Krajnik
Book Design: Michael Flynn

Photo Credits: Cover (car) Milos Vucicevic/Shutterstockcom; cover, p. 1 (emblem) Roberto Lusso/Shutterstock.com; cover, pp. 1, 3–6, 8, 10, 12–18, 20–22, 24, 26–32 (background) fotomak/Shutterstock.com; p. 5 (main) https://en.wikipedia.org/wiki/ALFA_40/60_HP#/media/File:Car_Mus%C3%A9e_Enzo_Ferrari_0002.JPG; p. 5 (Enzo Ferrari) https://en.wikipedia.org/wiki/Enzo_Ferrari#/media/File:Enzo_Ferrari_-_Wheel_of_a_racing_car.jpg; pp. 7, 9 (33 Stradale), 23 (main) Ion Sebastian/Shutterstock.com; p. 9 (4C Spider) Sergey Kohl/Shutterstock.com; p. 11 (main) Karlis Dambrans/Shutterstock.com; p. 11 (Giulia GTA) Rodrigo Garrido/Shutterstock.com; p. 12 https://it.wikipedia.org/wiki/Alfa_Romeo_TZ3#/media/File:Alfa_Romeo_TZ3_Corsa_by_Zagato_-_Flickr_-_exfordy.jpg; p. 13 Allan Hamilton/Icon Sportswire/Getty Images; p. 15 dimcars/Shutterstock.com; p. 17 Rust/ullstein bild/Getty Images; pp. 19 (main), 25 (main) Art Konovalov/Shutterstock.com; p. 19 (engine) https://en.wikipedia.org/wiki/JTS_engine#/media/File:Alfa_Romeo_Brera_V6_engine.JPG; p. 20 Chromatic Studio/Shutterstock.com; p. 21 Grzegorz Czapski/Shutterstock.com; p. 23 (inset) Maksim Toome/Shutterstock.com; p. 25 (inset) Dong liu/Shutterstock.com; p. 27 Auto BILD Syndication/ullstein bild/Getty Images; pp. 28–29 cristiano barni/Shutterstock.com.

Cataloging-in-Publication Data

Names: Kingston, Seth.
Title: The history of Alfa Romeos / Seth Kingston.
Description: New York : PowerKids Press, 2019. | Series: Under the hood | Includes glossary and index.
Identifiers: ISBN 9781538344484 (pbk.) | ISBN 9781538343364 (library bound) | ISBN 9781538344491 (6 pack)
Subjects: LCSH: Alfa Romeo automobile–Juvenile literature.
Classification: LCC TL215.A35 K56 2019 | DDC 629.222-dc23

Manufactured in the United States of America

CPSIA Compliance Information: Batch #CWPK19: For Further Information contact Rosen Publishing, New York, New York at 1-800-237-9932

CONTENTS

A CENTURY OF INNOVATION 4
ALFA TO ALFA ROMEO 6
DESIGN FIRST 8
MODERN ALFA ROMEOS 10
CELEBRATING 100 YEARS 12
ALFA ROMEO AND FORMULA ONE 14
THE DUETTO 16
THE BRERA: COMPACT YET POWERFUL 18
THE GIULIETTA: REVISITING A CLASSIC 20
A LIMITED EDITION DESIGN 22
COMBINING HISTORY AND PRACTICALITY 24
THE 159: A COMPACT EXECUTIVE CAR 26
DESIGNS FOR THE FUTURE 28
TIMELINE 30
GLOSSARY 31
INDEX 32
WEBSITES 32

A CENTURY OF INNOVATION

Alfa Romeo is an Italian car manufacturer known for its luxury sports cars. It's one of the oldest and most successful sports car makers in the world. Even though Alfa Romeo has had its ups and downs throughout its almost 110-year history, the company has stayed in business for so long because it places a great deal of importance on **innovation** and eye-catching **design**.

Alfa Romeo isn't only **legendary** for its cars. The company is also known for its racing successes. Soon after the company was founded, Alfa Romeo began participating in motor racing. Since then, Alfa Romeos have competed in a number of different styles of racing, including Formula One. Alfa Romeo has also built engines for other racing teams.

> IN 1914, GIUSEPPE MEROSI DESIGNED THE ALFA 40-60 GRAND PRIX, OR GP, BASED ON THE 40-60 HP, WHICH WAS ALSO ONE OF HIS DESIGNS, TO BREAK INTO THE INTERNATIONAL RACING SCENE.

||| START YOUR ENGINES |||

IN 1929, ENZO FERRARI, WHO STARTED DRIVING FOR ALFA ROMEO IN 1920, FOUNDED THE SCUDERIA FERRARI RACING TEAM IN MODENA, ITALY. HE LATER WENT ON TO CREATE HIS OWN CAR COMPANY—FERRARI.

ENZO FERRARI

ALFA TO ALFA ROMEO

On June 24, 1910, Alfa Romeo began as a company called Anonima Lombarda Fabbrica Automobili or ALFA, located near Milan, Italy. That year, ALFA released its first car—the 24 HP. Giuseppe Merosi, who had previously designed cars for Fiat, designed the 24 HP. The 24 HP could reach a top speed of 62 miles (99.7 km) per hour. On February 3, 1918, ALFA became publicly owned and was registered under a new name—Alfa Romeo.

In 1961, Alfa Romeo began **exporting** cars to the United States. The first car to come to the United States was the Giulietta. Alfa Romeos were sold in the United States and Canada until 1995. Alfa Romeo officially resumed selling cars in the United States in 2008.

IN 1954, ALFA ROMEO LAUNCHED ONE OF ITS MOST LEGENDARY CARS—THE GIULIETTA—WITH THE SPRINT **VERSION**.

DESIGN FIRST

In Alfa Romeo's early years, a strong **emphasis** was put on designing cars for racing. One of Alfa Romeo's primary designers, Giuseppe Merosi, created some of the company's first successful race cars. However, after Nicola Romeo took over the company in 1915 and World War I ended in 1918, Vittorio Jano came in to design lighter, more powerful cars.

Over the years, Alfa Romeo began creating cars known for their performance on the racetrack and their ability to double as family cars. Many are known for their classic designs. Today's Alfa Romeos are designed for people who want a performance car but also want safety

A REMINDER OF A LIFE LOST

Driver Ugo Sivocci died in 1923 while testing a new race car at the Monza racetrack. This car, unlike his others, didn't have his lucky *quadrifoglio* (a four-leaf clover on a white square) on it. After this, to honor Sivocci's life, a triangle with a four-leaf clover on it has appeared on all Alfa Romeo race cars. The missing corner of the original square stands for the loss of Sivocci.

4C SPIDER

33 STRADALE

MODERN ALFA ROMEOS

In 2018, Alfa Romeo sold four different models in the United States. They were a high-performance SUV called the Stelvio, a sedan (a car that has four doors and room for four or more people) called the Giulia, and two performance cars called the 4C Coupe and 4C Spider.

Each of these vehicles has a number of different choices, from the standard, to the Ti (which stands for Turismo internationale), to the Quadrifoglio. The customer can make changes to their car with different packages, paint colors, and more.

The Stelvio is more of a family car but can be changed for higher performance. The Giulia features more of a racing style and handles well on the road. The 4C is a less expensive six-speed automatic that is light and speedy.

TODAY, ONLY THE QUADRIFOGLIO MODELS OF NEW ALFA ROMEOS AND ALFA ROMEO RACE CARS HAVE THE QUADRIFOGLIO ON THEM. THIS IS ANOTHER EXAMPLE OF ALFA ROMEO'S CLASSIC DESIGNS.

THE GIULIA

In 1962, Alfa Romeo launched the Giulia family of cars, which had tested well in a wind tunnel in Turin, Italy. These cars were more aerodynamic, or moved through the air more easily, than other cars in their class. The first model to be released was the Giulia Ti. Like the Giulietta, the Giulia came in a number of models, including the Ti Super, 1300, and Nuova Super. In 1965, Alfa Romeo released the Giulia GTA, which stands for Gran Turismo Alleggerita. In 1966, 1967, and 1968, a Giulia GTA won the European Touring Car Championship.

GIULIA GTA

CELEBRATING 100 YEARS

Race cars aren't meant for everyday driving. In 2010, Alfa Romeo launched the Zagato TZ3 Corsa, built to celebrate Alfa Romeo's 100th anniversary of racing. A German collector named Martin Kapp **commissioned** this one-of-a-kind race car. Nine units of the Alfa Romeo TZ3 Stradale, which is the road version of the TZ3 Corsa, were also built to celebrate Alfa Romeo's 100th anniversary on the road.

IN 2010, THE TZ3 CORSA WON THE VILLA D'ESTE DESIGN **CONCEPT** AWARD.

GIULIA TZ

The Zagato TZ3 Corsa is based on the Giulia TZ, which Alfa Romeo released in 1963. TZ stands for Tubolare Zagato. *Tubolare*, or "tubular" in Italian, refers to the car's chassis, or supporting frame. Zagato refers to the company that designed the Giulia TZ. In its first year of racing, the Giulia TZ won several races in Europe and North America.

ALFA ROMEO AND FORMULA ONE

Alfa Romeo has been racing almost since the day it produced its first car. Racing is very important for sports car companies. It gives them a chance to use the latest **technology** in motorsports **engineering**. Alfa Romeo has competed in many types of races. It has raced in Formula Three races, rally races, and touring races such as the World Touring Car Championship.

In 1950, Nino Farina won Alfa Romeo's first Formula One championship at Silverstone, England. Farina raced an Alfa Romeo 158, which Gioacchino Colombo designed. His teammate Manuel Fangio took second place. In 1951, Fangio won the Alfa Romeo's second Formula One World championship in an Alfa Romeo 159. Fangio is known as one of the greatest Formula One drivers of all time.

THE ALFA ROMEO 158 AND ITS UPDATE THE 159 ARE SOME OF THE MOST SUCCESSFUL RACING CARS OF ALL TIME. THESE CARS GOT THE NICKNAME ALFETTA, WHICH MEANS "LITTLE ALFA" IN ITALIAN.

||| START YOUR ENGINES |||

THE 159 WAS NICKNAMED THE "GODDESS OF LOVE" BECAUSE IT COULD FILL THE DRIVER WITH FEELINGS OF LOVE FOR BEING ON THE ROAD.

THE DUETTO

In March 1966, the Alfa Romeo Spider was launched at the 36th Geneva Motor Show. At that point, the car didn't have a name. Alfa Romeo held a contest to see who could come up with the best name for the car. The winning name was Duetto, which means "duet" in Italian. Alfa Romeo couldn't legally call the car the Duetto because a chocolate snack already had the name. The car's official name is the Alfa Romeo Spider 1600.

Made from 1966 to 1993, the Spider is one of the most-loved Alfa Romeos ever created. It was also the longest-running model of Alfa Romeo. Pininfarina, a famous Italian design company, designed the Spider as a convertible. However, some models of the Spider were available as hardtops. Pininfarina also designed the Giulietta Spider for Alfa Romeo as well as cars for Ferrari, Lamborghini, and many others.

DURING ITS 27 YEARS OF PRODUCTION, ONLY MINOR CHANGES WERE MADE TO THE DESIGN AND **MECHANICS** OF THE ALFA ROMEO SPIDER.

||| START YOUR ENGINES |||

THE DUETTO WAS FEATURED IN THE 1967 MOVIE *THE GRADUATE*, WHICH STARRED DUSTIN HOFFMAN. THE CAR THAT WAS USED IN THE FILM WAS SOLD IN THE UNITED STATES.

1966 SPIDER DUETTO

THE BRERA
COMPACT YET POWERFUL

Alfa Romeo produced the Brera from 2005 to 2010. It was a three-door, 2+2 coupe, which means it had two front seats and two rear seats. Giorgetto Giugiaro of Italdesign-Giugiaro designed the Brera, and Pininfarina built each of the Brera's 21,786 units. The Brera was originally going to be Alfa Romeo's reintroduction into the U.S. market. However, Alfa Romeo decided not to export the Brera.

The Brera combined classic Alfa Romeo design with a powerful punch. It debuted at the 2005 Geneva Motor Show, when it was also announced a Spider version would be available. The 2009 Brera Q4 could go from 0 to 60 miles (0 to 96.6 km) per hour in 6.8 seconds. Its top speed was 139 miles (223.7 km) per hour.

> IN 2009, ALFA ROMEO PARTNERED WITH ITALIA INDEPENDENT, AN ITALIAN DESIGN COMPANY, TO RELEASE A LIMITED EDITION OF THE BRERA AND SPIDER. ONLY 900 UNITS WERE MADE.

BRERA ENGINE

THE GIULIETTA
REVISITING A CLASSIC

In 1954, Alfa Romeo launched the Giulietta with the Sprint. Almost 28,000 units of this model were sold. The Giulietta came in a number of different options: the Berlina, Ti, Sprint and Spider (both of which came in a Veloce model), Sprint Speciale, and Sprint Zagato. The Spider model was released in 1955. It was created because a U.S. company had taken interest in the car and ordered 600 units. In 1961, Alfa Romeo celebrated the sale of 100,001 units of the Giulietta.

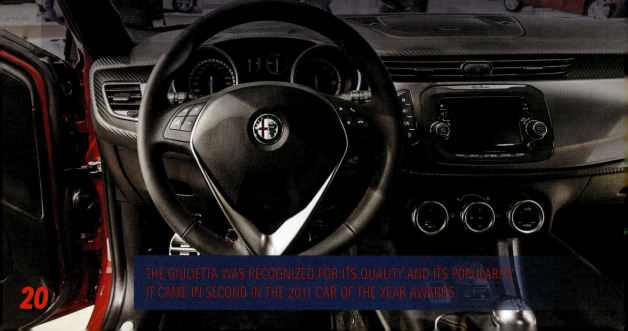

THE GIULIETTA WAS RECOGNIZED FOR ITS QUALITY AND ITS POPULARITY. IT CAME IN SECOND IN THE 2011 CAR OF THE YEAR AWARDS.

The Giulietta was reintroduced in 2010. It replaced an earlier model, called the 147, and its design was based on the Giulietta Sprint Veloce. The 2010 Alfa Romeo Giulietta was a five-door hatchback designed to be a stylish, small family car.

A LIMITED EDITION DESIGN

Alfa Romeo debuted the 8C Competizione at the 2003 Frankfurt Motor Show as a concept car. During the 2006 Paris Auto Show, Alfa Romeo announced it would produce a limited number of the 8C Competizione.

The 8C Competizione was a limited edition touring car named for its eight **cylinders**. This modern Alfa Romeo was created to honor the racing traditions of the 1930s and featured a V-8 engine.

The Competizione came in two versions: a coupe and a spider. The 8C Competizione coupe was produced from 2007 to 2009. The spider was produced from 2008 to 2010. Only 500 each of the coupe and the spider were made. The 8C Competizione marked Alfa Romeo's return to exporting to the United States after pulling out in 1995.

ONLY 35 8C COMPETIZIONE SPIDERS WERE SOLD IN THE UNITED STATES COMPARED TO 84 COUPES.

COMBINING
HISTORY AND PRACTICALITY

At the 2008 British Motor Show, Alfa Romeo introduced the MiTo, a three-door supermini, which is a car larger than a city car but smaller than a small family car. Alfa Romeo held a competition to name the car, and the winning name was Furiosa. However, Alfa Romeo decided to name the car MiTo, which is a shortened form of the Italian cities of Milano (Milan), where the car was designed, and Torino (Turin), where the car was assembled.

Alfa Romeo is known for its powerful sports cars, but the MiTo is a small car made for city driving. The MiTo is noticeably less powerful than most Alfa Romeos but powerful compared to other cars its size. The MiTo was the first Alfa Romeo to have a DNA system, which allows the driver to switch between driving settings depending on road conditions.

THE MITO HAS A 1.4-LITER ENGINE AND A TOP SPEED OF 134 MILES (215.7 KM) PER HOUR. IT CAN GO FROM 0 TO 60 MILES (0 TO 96.6 KM) PER HOUR IN 8 SECONDS.

THE 159
A COMPACT EXECUTIVE CAR

At the 2005 Geneva Motor Show, Alfa Romeo launched the Alfa Romeo 159, a compact executive car, which is a smaller luxury car. The 159 replaced the 156 and was built on the same platform—or a shared set of common design, engineering, and production efforts—as the Alfa Romeo Brera and Spider.

The 159 came in two different styles—a four-door sedan and a five-door station wagon. The station wagon, called the 159 Sportwagon, was first shown at the 2006 Geneva Motor Show. Even though the Sportwagon was a family-friendly car, it also had the power for which Alfa Romeo is known.

In 2007, 2009, and 2010, the 159 competed in the Bathurst 12 Hour, an endurance race that takes place near Bathurst, Australia. In 2009, it placed first in its class.

THE ALFA ROMEO 159 WON A NUMBER OF AWARDS, INCLUDING THE 2006 AUTO BILD DESIGN AWARD AND THE 2006 FLEET WORLD HONOURS DESIGN AWARD.

ııı START YOUR ENGINES ııı

TWO BLACK 159s WERE USED IN *QUANTUM OF SOLACE*, A JAMES BOND FILM, IN 2008. THEY WERE USED IN THE OPENING SCENES AND IN THE CAR CHASE SCENE.

DESIGNS FOR THE FUTURE

With its updated lineup of cars in the United States, Alfa Romeo is positioned to continue as one of the most sought-after sports car manufacturers. Known for its design-forward approach, Alfa Romeo's performance cars show that the company isn't stuck in the past but working hard to create cars for the future.

ALFA ROMEOS CONTINUE TO PARTICIPATE IN FORMULA ONE RACING AS PART OF TEAM SAUBER FERRARI, WHICH RACES ALFA ROMEO C37s.

Collectors continue to show older models of Alfa Romeos at classic car shows. Car lovers have the chance to see the newest Alfa Romeo designs and concepts displayed at car shows around the world.

Today, Alfa Romeo focuses primarily on designing sports cars that appeal not only to serious car **enthusiasts** but also to families and people who drive in cities. The cars that made the company a serious **contender** more than a century ago are the inspiration for future Alfa Romeos.

TIMELINE

June 24, 1910 ❯ ALFA is established outside Milan, Italy.

1910 ❯ ALFA creates the 24 HP.

1914 ❯ Giuseppe Merosi designs the ALFA 40–60 GP.

February 3, 1918 ❯ Alfa Romeo goes public.

1920 ❯ Enzo Ferrari begins racing for Alfa Romeo.

1954 ❯ Alfa Romeo launches the Giulietta.

1961 ❯ Alfa Romeo begins exporting cars to the United States.

1962 ❯ Alfa Romeo launches the Giulia family of cars.

1966 ❯ Alfa Romeo launches the Spider.

1995 ❯ Alfa Romeo stops exporting cars to the United States.

2003 ❯ Alfa Romeo debuts the 8C Competizione concept car.

2005 ❯ Alfa Romeo launches the Brera.

2005 ❯ Alfa Romeo launches the 159.

2008 ❯ Alfa Romeo launches the MiTo.

2010 ❯ Alfa Romeo launches the Zagato TZ3 Corsa.

2010 ❯ Alfa Romeo reintroduces the Giulietta.

2018 ❯ Alfa Romeo sells four models in the United States—the Stelvio, the Giulia, the 4C Coupe, and the 4C Spider.

GLOSSARY

commission: To order or request something to be made or done.

concept: Organized around a main idea or theme; created to show a general idea.

contender: A person who is in competition with others.

cylinder: A tube-shaped part of an engine where power is created.

design: The way something has been made. Also, to create the plan for something.

emphasis: Special attention or importance given to something.

engineering: The study and practice of using math and science to do useful things, such as building machines.

enthusiast: Someone passionate about a certain hobby or subject.

export: To send a product to another country to sell it.

innovation: A new way of doing things.

legendary: Very famous because of special qualities or abilities.

mechanics: The way something works or things are done.

technology: The way people do something and the tools they use.

version: A form of something that is different from the ones that came before it.

INDEX

A
Alfa Romeo 159, 14, 15, 26, 27, 30
Alfa Romeo Spider 1600, 16, 26, 30

B
Brera, 18, 19, 26, 30

D
Duetto, 16

E
8C Competizione, 22, 30

F
Formula One, 4, 14, 28
4C Coupe, 8, 10, 30
4C Spider, 8, 9, 10, 30

G
Giulia, 10, 11, 13, 30
Giulietta, 6, 16, 20, 21, 30

M
MiTo, 24, 30

P
Pininfarina, 16, 18

S
Sportwagon, 26
Sprint, 20
Stelvio, 10, 30

T
33 Stradale, 8, 9
24 HP, 6, 30

Z
Zagato TZ3 Corsa, 12, 13, 30

WEBSITES

Due to the changing nature of Internet links, PowerKids Press has developed an online list of websites related to the subject of this book. This site is updated regularly. Please use this link to access the list: www.powerkidslinks.com/hood/romeos